Have you seen the Crocodile?
First published in England by Walker Books Ltd, London.
Copyright © 1986 by Colin West
Printed in Hong Kong. All rights reserved.
Library of Congress Catalog Card No. 85-45747
ISBN 0-06-443101-0
First Harper Trophy edition, 1986. Reprinted 1991
Published in hardcover by J. B. Lippincott, New York

HAVE YOU SEEN THE
CROCODILE?

Story and pictures by
Colin West

A Harper Trophy Book
Harper & Row, Publishers

'Have you seen the crocodile?'
asked the parrot.

'No,'
said the
dragonfly.

'Have you seen the crocodile?'
asked the parrot
and the dragonfly.

'No,'
said the
bumble bee.

'Have you seen the crocodile?'
asked the parrot
and the dragonfly
and the bumble bee.

'No,'
said the
butterfly.

'Have you seen the crocodile?'
asked the parrot
and the dragonfly
and the bumble bee
and the butterfly.

'No,' said the hummingbird.

'Have you seen the crocodile?'
asked the parrot
and the dragonfly
and the bumble bee
and the butterfly
and the hummingbird.

'No,' said the frog.

'No one's seen the crocodile!'
said the parrot
and the dragonfly
and the bumble bee
and the butterfly
and the hummingbird
and the frog.

But then…

'I'VE SEEN THE CROCODILE!'
snapped the crocodile.

'Have YOU seen the parrot
and the dragonfly
and the bumble bee
and the butterfly
and the hummingbird
and the frog?'

asked the crocodile.